Invent This!

By

Zeeshan Mahmud

Creativity Workbook
No. 4

ACKNOWLEDGEMENT

My thanks to every photographer whose work I used from Pexels.

Invent a magic trick where a man is forced to think of this card after being flashed it in the street.

Invent an enlightenment paradise: a place guaranteed to provide satori.

Invent a VR component that gives one a bird's eye view of an astral travel journey.

Invent a story whereby entering a parrish the soul becomes the embodiment of the building.

Create your portrait.... in the dark!

Master a subject by blasting through 40 books on that topic speed reading at page a second.

Code an enlightenment software.

Manifest.

Design an augmented reality algorithm that will teleport you to any country instantaneously.

Create a ballet routine for an amoeba.

Create a device that will force the subconscious mind to change a paradigm...guaranteed!

Write an algorithm that will teach a pupil to distinguish between shades of color.

Create a studio "Virtual Zero" where a single chamber encodes different versions of augmented reality.

Invent a humanoid robot that can levitate for a pizza company named "Otherworld".

Invent an algorithm that comes up with unique brand of magic and illusion to teach others.

Invent a filtered helmet that momentarily "switches off" a color.

Invent a free diving program that incentivizes by planting real pearl!

Invent a story whereby a washing machine complex gains sentience and recruits workers in accelerated fashion to train them just under an hour to work for it so as to take over the world.

Invent a chart that determines your level of astigmatism just from this painting!

Invent a phone that literally opens up a new dimensional world and let you transcend reality.

Invent a methodology of blind spot detection system of a powerplant that justifiably measures the level with a metric value.

Invent a mixer that effectively uploads all of a person's lifetime of photos, videos and fragments to create a short four minute flashy music video.